MW00397266

This book belongs to:

____